Lure

Heller Levinson

BLACK WIDOW PRESS

Boston, MA

Black Widow Press is an imprint of Commonwealth Books, Inc., Boston, MA. Distributed to the trade by NBN (National Book Network) throughout North America, Canada, and the U.K. All Black Widow Press books are printed on acid-free paper, and glued into bindings. Black Widow Press and its logo are registered trademarks of Commonwealth Books, Inc.

Joseph S. Phillips and Susan J. Wood, Ph.D., Publishers
www.blackwidowpress.com

Cover design: Linda Lynch
Layout: Kerrie Kemperman
Cover art: Linda Lynch, *Untitled Oil Study,* Oil on paper,
20 x 15 inches, 2021
Photo: Penina Meisels
Page 98: Linda Lynch, *Barque,* Pastel pigment on cotton paper,
60 x 44 inches, 2019
Page 127: Linda Lynch, *After Turmoil,* Pastel pigment on cotton paper,
30 x 22 inches, 2022
Photos: Marty Snortum

ISBN-13: 978-1-7371603-6-6
Printed in the United States
10 9 8 7 6 5 4 3 2 1

Lure

wish you were here

‘Language leads to language beyond dictionaries, references, and meanings. Meaning does not evaporate but is irreducible to signification: It is a form.’

— Octavio Paz

‘It is not meanings but the combinations among linguistic elements that produce a meaning beyond meaning.’

— Octavio Paz

‘All that matters here is that the boundaries drawn should not be too definite.’

— Kandinsky

‘Live free, child of the mist – and with respect to knowledge we are all children of the mist.’

— Thoreau

‘Less than a drop of my blood remains which does not tremble. I know the signs of the ancient flame.’

— Dante

‘Still forms are the negation of life, formulas and laws spread rigidity over the face of nature, numbers make dead.’

— Oswald Spengler

snowfed

whelped on fir

& manganese

conversant

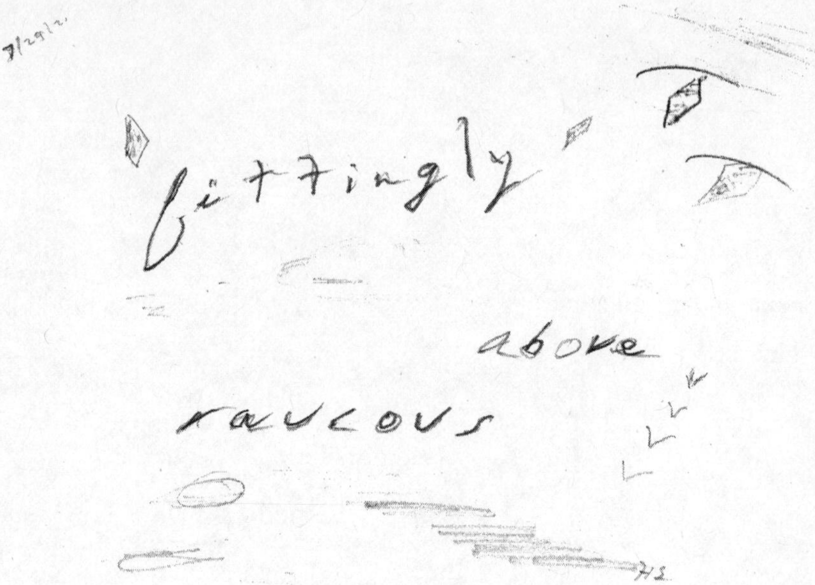

7/29/21
fittingly
above
raucous
HS

ravaging gauntcoiled fistblade

vestibule spin   larkfin

upend ,

..u t t e r

the company of cards

clutter

multiform pliancy

cherished opacity prevail veil

trill cere

lozenge wave

LUREINDELICATE trammeltrumped

truculent

teem

in the loftweld of febrile itinerancy

indiscretion

oversight

web wobble

paring latticework lungecraft

elongates rehearses

intervals

lure imminently

painstaking   purification by

means of resist

lodgecraft   ideology

retrofitting as a pursuit mechanism

sum of the parts

troubling for treble

the bass

well-contained

plangent like altitudinous thrush

tuft graven,   scarce, . . .

          blear drive gyration clutch,   ,

   , archipelago . . .

plaint catacomb remonstrate

beam bent loath-

ing no longer toothsome

ravages

going home

in the tiered bivouac of a slant obscurity

rupture bleed scant disclose

gnarl pittance cleat dissension

cleared for take-off stumble

cross-bred irregularity

capacity

culture

vulture rain, gnat tooth

from the thrombotic rumble of torn

reports this everlastingness

effer-vesces

GLOOM

wrinkle wrest scrummed

bedlam bled

puckered

gangly with Argentina

with bloat

accursed dodge angular dissolve

caliginous crank carbuncular

corky

gutted

anvil bludgeon

vacuumed by

ceremonial

brood

ABEYANCE

pause correlative gap

interstice

idle

elide

depart → lift → fr-

ay border peel scrap consort

s — t — r —i — p

dis—engage

meander

from radical stretch this gambit

this indispose

sup—

pressed inclination

lapse laurel

truancy

acts of kindness

plangent in disharmonious arrest

crud catalectic   disquiet

dearth crystal   lapse pugnacity

curdle

corrugate

contagion

conclusivity stripped   pier-

ced

emptiness emp-

ties

shallows concave

horizon planed . . .

kno-

ts

LURE

petition spool sift

ruffle

d a n d e l i o n

tra-

peze

motion sockets

eyelets

castanets

along with the rhumba the bouillabaisse the

abracadabra

MAROON

strained through silhouette

cupboarded, . . .

shorn,

nuptialed desolate

riven outlier

plied with excise

stripped of ex-

cess

bur -

geon

croons

how much of

lost

is

find

how much of

find

is

transparent

INCLEMENCY

pock-pit pitch gnarl forfeiture

. the subject was pitiful

. a table of manners

. trash removal

fugitive

furtive

déraciné

ARRAY

bear   to bear   bring forth

display

ar-range

how much of

array

is

arrangement

poetry: the art of arrangement

arrangement: the art of bringing forth, revelating

Son House: John The Revelator

where in the presentation is the decimal. punctuation arrays.

how much 'bringing forth' froths from *dis-array*?

Cannonball Adderley: Know what I mean, know what I mean?

adjudication. storm clouds. punctuality. mischief.

transit systems

ecumenical

customs

short time ago

DRIFT

loaf lassitudinous loll meander

filigree felicity feline fellatio

sunder be, . . . don't be-long

quittance burl bravado

en — ter — prise

away without *toward*

elongate *alongée* *ausdehnen* *allungare*

sough

serpentine

sizzle

DODGE

divert ditch skirt

absolve (?) dissolve (?)

declivitous

U-turn

disperse

where in the

dodge

is the

implicate

in the churn yaw of glistening dogleg →

abandon

stray dizen

brazen perplexity

proud water

STRAY

meander roam   rill-like : rivulet

like: ricochet   carnival   carousel

c a r o u s e

implicate

avert

intransitive

in the company of odds   heartfelt   genuflect   fleckspatter

feckless

flounder

flare   im-

peril   imperialism   loot forlorn

a-flutter   barrel rotund undulate

luxe

beer garden

in the lure of mermaid mes-

merism		wooly meander		solicitous glissade

li—

quid languidity		lush-loll		loft

laze libidinous

how much of

lure

is

fascination (fasten ; pull-to ; spool-through; absorb)

how much of

fascination

is

exoticism

fin ://: sin

The mermaid tail should not be critically compared to the Chinese practice of foot binding.

The mermaid tail drips with allure, with capacity, — *slick sickle splash* — swaggers potency, motile transpiration

how much of mermaid tail resembles phallic omnipotence

where are the flat-chested mermaids?

why do S-words love mermaids?

squiggly sea-plant   swish succubus

scrolling zippered shores

morsel-

bound

JOLLY

death spattered through

time's reek,

odor complexes construe con-

catenate resound

carelessnesses gripped by

bushwhack comply,

circumambulate

laden with

distill,

the un-

sightly

espy

LOST

déracine   uproot   *scald*

armature dissent diacritical collapse grid cataract *q u e a – sy*

attenuate moor dissolve soused by the

dialectics of ice house how

much of

renown

is

known

partings accrue   dev-

olutions

regenerate

lure invidious

aped salubrity   gloom domed

razed by the tatter rag of botched

suspension →

shutter

mold

fungi

claw asperity early arrivals unalarmed ro-

bed libidinous, aglut, transparent,

unfavorable odds, the man said,

play on

shareholding privileges strong shoulders how much of

the bearable is durable   restraints fail

oblivion played off-key sounds like

another chance

it wasn't obvious

BLUDGEON

early lunar

sow-bellied lethargies

cream adumbrates

worn salutes arrive uninvited

painstaking decimations

larkspur

once lovely

ALOFT

aerial   plié   suspend   *lift*

lived fictions the hardest to let go

cuffed deadlock   days spread anvil

sky with its back turned

the uppermost

rising

in the oft-wend of collapsed circumference

wizard-blitz tether-churn

cinder-whiff

barrel-hog

blister pyramidal skylark color

the song . . . wag purple foxglove broom-

bush juniper coconut oil

yank the sky-cleft upend

yearn burn privilege thistle

heart break the upright bass evenings

by the

lake

fireside

EVANESCENCE

irretrievable   sough-ed   porous

tripwire   furlough   *Slip*

presentation's ostentation

transpire

leak

ESTRANGE

addled dispense lurid carboniferous

sunk alliance *de*-brief

declivitous decline dethrone

p a r s e

facets smear eaves

of footprint →

erasure, fade, — fracture

, the rent that swallows

that heaves *Un*-stitch, flirt

reckon, slack slip-a

way slip-page

slippery skids the steadfast,

sullies the vernacular

from flame roof

exposure

INSTIGATORY

well-up flare incite

agitate

bundle bristle cleat clamp cracklepop

dart

cornerstone mortar sweep stairwell clearwater

elevate

parsnips hors d'oeuvres slick tires rucksack airline tickets

camouflage

commingle

suburbs shuffle nomenclature upstart flywheel grind gran-

diose

clackety-clack

when   appetites slather

in-iquities-equities lingo lango langoustine quiet *repose* time of

flooze flowsy temperance temporarily heraldry hurriedly

comeuppance bring a cup broadly brandy molasses bennies

ticklish measured occupancy Tangiers in the Fall

Constantinople anytime Mardi Gras tambourine tangerine ink

spots apple pick dark coffee too much of a good thing godly

grateful gratitude qualifications qualify quantifications deify

on a clear day you can see . . . fledge the gosling goose the

moose a cherry let loose spare change leave the earth alone

pontifications aside what do you do in your spare time is

spare time your rare time define rare are rare & special the

same? similar? till query do us cease just off the starboard

around the bend turn the corner far away further the matter

was laid to rest   news creates weather hard to dress for

preparation the keynote speaker let us all rise put your hands

to feel too much caution is incurable cartoons run amok what

can the matter be

IMPLICATE

subcutaneous   lurk lurid

tread inflammatory under-

size

sunk syllable

through a relinquished callisthenic muscular re-

bar   hush money

attention to vowels when

consonants carry

the song

EMPTY RATTLE

far off   further

                    clench beyond

                              beyond earthenware

                                        dawn distinction

                                                  capillary

ecstatic eidolons rove vac-

uumed warrens, bleached forest,

shed river

hallucinogens wrest corporeal in

balletic snicker, finger

crushed cinder, bled morsel,

arboreal rictus, crank

calumny

dating alliterates time,

funds orchestration,

bellows the plume of a

spent

abbreviation

of a

drilled

abscess

when absenteeism no longer a

flaw but representation an allude a point

to an embark a nullity-reek in the

'who's there' of elimination – the company

of kings the treasury department armoires

mercantilism – annulments conflagrate

collide, borders, stripped of purpose,

mull vacuity's insistence, the

peevishness of

desolate,

the

perpetuity

of

hollow

SPLAY

splash around   abut abound

veer part oblong   obliquity

disproportionate harmonic

a beehive contesting   lovers in

asynchronous unravel   few & far

between   mountable   discourse

on purple

. wasn't always like this

. could have been otherwise

. please say you will

DEVIATION

detour divagate   digress

                    dismiss   disengage   diverge

                                                                        sever

bungle

          abrogate

                    abnegate

    how much of

    deviate

    is

    devastate

in the slingfrost of otherwise

brambledamp

in the wend-weft-whir of human kind I climb these

steps,

. . . alone,

. . . petrified

when **considerations peel**

to stone pliancy issues stakes

claim feedback loops leaflets underwater

arrest

comfort levers inutile, malposed,

buffoonery best serves propaganda

weary catch-alls

render, innocent of

navigation,

resplend,

. . .

blur

in the shadow-lag of nitrogen bobcat

vitreous glissando   slur parade

          rack destiny

premature usurp griddles windless tomes

fumbles binomials

from the birthing stains of charismatic slippage

meridian stutter   pharmaceutical cunctation   cock-

tail blemish

the ruse widens

faraways

loosen

shadow stravage

unsealed unsubstantiated

peeled from surface

gone askew chortling

unstrung

a shadow un-folding

re-

composing as

non-affiliate

a lurk

in consummate

consideration

Shadow Secrete

succulence skirmish spray

in the off-fling light-suck of colorless lurk

host renegade

identity hijack

supplementary friction

furtive incorporeal freighted

with

obstinacy

with pools

of

plot

Shadow Sinister

unkempt exacerbate   dodge dartful

gall-whetted blear mu-ling wildebeest brood

from the soma of outskirt taren-

tella taunt

mink slippage

marled ruse

festering in the lure of rainbowed nullity

sullen-soused shudder bled of

rodomontade of stapled mnemonics

transferable for oar

        for

hirsute gala

      for

adulterate

row

Shadow Sustain

petaled out   unruffled foretaste em-

bedment

pond immaculate

frog felicitous lilium lambent fracture foil

glissade

rotate

inordinate

afar off

reclamation

rustle

Shadow Disjunct

lopped   isolate abrade

lone cast-off

Nubian maroon

truncate

truant

ripped

source-torn paled expatriate musing incorporeal declension

formidable forbear

formulates autonomy

ripples with the

reek

of

slippage

World becomes World

through Word

SLIPPAGE

drilled metric		species crumble

	trapeze freeze		anaconda prance

hoisting forgotten barbs through hoops of quarantine

dread speculation

wobbly icon

dismembered machinery

corroded tunnels funnel bled category	rampant embolism

	stale currency		botched script

from the halls of séance

the

unheard

Spill As Maturating Slippage

slur impregnate eke-through edge-

along

        l

                e

                        a

                                k

                                        slide lark

lubricious extrude

advanced insinuation

SINKAGE

down dove drill decline declen-

sion brood bore

barrel braid

plummet

abrade

deliquesce

forego

when all else arises

fable flicker jackpot ways & means the Supremes 'Stop! In

The Name of Love' overture applause skirt the tally tuck the

fissure Giant

Steps go goosey live eels for sale platter paste stash

away bargain chips let it fell rain slip salsa abdominal pain

puddles vodka

vermouth velvet the trial of Edie Lang inconsistency breath

long legs connivance gullies gallows raisins corn stalk

carnivorous

hammocks afternoon

often

KNOT

intercoursing vocabularies ravel

revel protuberant   bundleclaspintertwine

bulb conversational cavort quidd-

ity commingle   strand coalesce

quanta   parcel jam friction flare accumu-

late

gather-swell

beryl

Lure Altitudinous

strip   taper   whittle   leaven   prune

                                                load perforate

shorn of . . .

drizzling through unkempt ringed with temperature pollen-

based   foliate float

                              buoyant

                                        weave-waft

                                                  trill-troll

fertile   wing woozy

ascensional demands

scriptural surplus

. acquisition as stunted flight response

. sophistry sliced into wafers

. allegiance as a lower order conditioning

. can the sinister dismiss its shadow?

. far-offs roamed as if there were no end in sight.

. is random truly random or misunderstood?

. does a commitment to gyration entail lucidity?

GYRATION

'We require something like a mental gyration on the heel. We need so rapid a revolution of all things about the central point of sight, that, while the minutiae vanish altogether even the more conspicuous objects become blended into one.'

from *Eureka,* E. A. Poe

seersight astral lyre fever kinetic threadout torque cycle boost

pre-allocational fitness loop centripetal urge skin-in

fringe hazard

wallop-stir

vertigo

sour calendrical

cyclotronic azure

sp-

in inject spur cylindrical concupiscence swirl synecdoche

sleave rollout sphere spiral rapprochement   Eur —

Eka *!*

SWARM

castoff percolate enormity heave-throws heft

driven wound in ventricular helium at the base of slippage

spool velocity cascade uplift cocoon undulate spiral bound

oath airing a singular voice meticulously

elaborate

when expiration depose

vapor evaporate the methodically empty

tinder-shorn

vacuumed

where a collapsed perpetuity

defuses

Abyssal Asylum

miter undercut subaltern fracture

isotope strew landbound leaden

gratuitous consensus cults grow que-

asy   querulous   pock

suspicious

weigh

weighted

eerily   down   drawn

duct tape

fallow

inner hydraulics

lethargy magnified

reduced to

infinitesimal subtraction

to

self-abnegating

calculi

lure demurely

enhanced archipelago   endear damask be-

guile   gully pond

fern frond

Hindemith/Debussy   Monet/Morandi

the mirage of modes   the

synecdoche of transparent

accessorize

sashay

Brood Asylum

ponderous rum pugnacity drill

deliberate   thick

glum cordon

web lactose

smear accumulate

braiding density loops   swoop

   swivel   roil lugubrious

      lowly slung

EDGE

spun filament preamble   precipice

        thinned   vanquished orthodoxy

spatialdecrescence   peakabbreviate

a furlough at odds

folds filiate sparse cilia

bunched with extremity

naked

wary

ABSENT

cutaway cull beleaguered mitigate

cross-sectional obliviate

circumscribe

empty

shelved ruminate

protracted delimit

embellished caesura

a proclivity

sur-

c

e

a

s

e

AERIAL

lift

sprite cylindrical scintilla loft

wax

terrestrial abnegate

swill cirrus stellar celerity

wisp-froth flotation

wand-waft

extracurricular cum-

ulous

AMBIENT

suffuse soak surplus

swell squall opulent

aerate

diffuse

accumulative dispersal

, immerse

the fetch of a thing luminesces

, draws , envelops ,

lubricates

osmoses

how much of

aura

is

evaporation

GRAVITY

'But from the sleeper falls

(as though from a motionless cloud)

the abundant rain of the heavy.'

inarticulate resined

rinsed garrulous

woodlands confer

when obstacles make it seem

unreasonable when inopportune   unseasonable with outwit

with dismay outweighed overburdened tromped stomped

popped shucked jived disfavored jammed discolored deflator

de-flavor hallelujah call Savior snap crack gee-whiz go dizzy

clop drop your skivvies jump jolly hop a' long steer the trolley

clap sing go ding ling ling   ain't got a chance? dazzle prance

hi-hat glance prince the streets go aberrant go crazy go

underground lurk seep spew postulate weep divvy the dander

go yonder ponder perilous ponder pomp ostentation & the

wobbly woo cinch carillon clairvoyant conveyor catch–all

cinder tender no surrender say

your piece

, please

how much of

maturity

is

reclamation

Abyssal Interrogation

plumb   probe lure cast

plummet skirl throb   annoin-

ted husks rumor the room

rummage shadows

rue

stone resoundings dim proposal

foundations faulty totter brink truck residual

haunts circumnavigate

pro-

vide periphery

lessness

shear dismantle mitigate tum-

ble abrogate

abrade

grind

Cioran writes:

'In English the French text Sans is called *Lessness,* a word coined by Beckett, as he coined the German equivalent *Losigkeit.*

This word *lessness* (as unfathomable as Boehme's *Ungrund*) so fascinated me that one evening I told him I would not sleep until I found an honorable French equivalent. . . . We considered together every possible form suggested by *sans* and *moindre.* None seemed to come close to the inexhaustible *lessness,* a mixture of privation and infinity, a vacuity synonymous with apotheosis.'

lessness: not a 'vacuity' but a dim, . . . an abate.

chipped away at reduced watercolor figment

memory:

is the memory less than the remembered?

the ghost of the loved one lives larger than the loved one live.

track the fade.

the vanish (vanquish ? ?)

absence out-presences presence.

lessness is not strictly correlative.

lessness: the not nothing that is not much.

ambiguity wobbles quantification, creates quagmire,

instability, . . . murk,

miasma, —

the pugnaciously dissipate unravels

in the dwindle dim slur of legendary drizzle, . . . sullen

ovation, lisped beguile,

swells

slippery

lure

splinter

from debilitative sunder this augment, this

wayfarer drift

is the fictive less than the real?

the shadow than the body?

the echo than original sound?

how much of

lessness

is

deflation?

evacuation ??

how many ways does lessness magnify?

visibility thaw migra —

tory vapor

suspire

depletive adorn

flense

peel,

. . .

.

Abyssal Cavort

frothway freeze-dried cauterize crimp

cataract loose change

pubic meander public slander

crest dividend spiral spin

chance

prance

cradle pinwheel pancreatic prance stay a while smither ye
bonkers good soil is rich in nutrients wish you were here
when it's over come to a decision before matters deteriorate to
the barely audible the rarely seen seam pockets dust jackets
overly populated barometric confusion according to
procedure
scantily clad but fulsome

NUGATORY

dart diminish   dispirit draw

  malfunction

    obviate

        deprive

the suitors wore trucks.

                                        transparency

                                  . backfired

        bareback provides superior

              contact.

      illustrious of alien is the cuttlefish.

         not too close not too far

          forthright furthermore

        won't you at the right moment

plume array cross junction superlative

permutations enliven sitting cross-legged

pleurisy in all its forms

companionship wears thin

scrutiny

in the curdle crust aftermath of

a spent conspiracy

        flotsam stew

        glandular swell

        ovaline

a blurred benignity trench fire foot scramble

baste proverbial

                scallop suds

                idiosyncratic water

hyperbole

lure in salubrious slumber

inundate disrobe scatter shutdown

slur, slide parade

simmer swell

diffuse

en—

sorcell

moisten

bounty stellar gloam nuzzle gussied slumber sartorial

calamitous dethrone repose respite

under-tow

gleam sonorous nightglue

bipedal loiter

nugget psalm

u-

biq-

uitous

face-to-face

cornerstone whimsy whorl salutation skirl center-

piece

'The tree and we meet one another, as the tree stands

and we stand face to face with it.'

affront ://: confront

confront → commingle/twine

where in the

face-to-face

is the

consort?

the

contort?

does the meet-up require resolution? would tactility tip the

scales?

> *perceptual tingle alight optic tango tremolo burn* <

topsytipsy entangle mesh

coil flex reverberate

does *in*-gest require breakdown?

meltdown?

swash flotate tryst tingle

throughfoil dispatch

tripping approximates boulder the chill,   flint

follicles for lash

The *S*pray notes (s) are intended to irrigate the text much as a fine mist recirculates to sea.

S The quoted matter (4th & 5th line) arises from Heidegger's What Is Called Thinking where how being with the tree differs from our 'idea' of the tree is explored: "This face-to-face meeting is not, then, one of these 'ideas' buzzing about in our heads."

through old growth ambulant pith

emmissarial legend heft practiced port de bras

                    round

observe,   grueled

obeisant, . . . tantamount truisms

sigil waft alarm,   predispose

an elastic lumber conversant with

imbalance, with

discretionary ineluctability plushed in the

cedar-thrall groin of

imperturbable

erectility

in the lustre lure of asynchronous spur

ambivalent molecules scramble scatter string spherical sunder

á posteriori axiomatic purblind muddle manifold

comeuppance critical   oxygenate   low tide prairie

swamp in the company of eider strategic meltdown synaptic

collapse crud curricula grasp hypertrophy, — flutter:

algae mind   reminiscent ice

        horizontal undulate

wave

in the lustre lure of asymmetric spar

rotational rupture   round serrate   bonewind

duck shadow

observation hallucinogenic hijack occlude

jack of all transmissions lone articulate uprouses spurious

tread measly

love knots rata tat tat calibrate rowel the armor of old men

sea froth allergenic hairpiece the luxury of non-compliance

have you bathed?

do you campaign much?

care for water?

in love. falling in love. always in. making a habit. of. love love love. in the of of love. lovely. falling. love being love being falling. tumbling stumbling bruising losing self hi diddle diddle stagger lee don't bruise your knee in the peril fling far flung love for all fall thrall. a ball. in the free fetter release. finite decease. on the way to love falling in love with love. loving Love spells Lovely. what can the matter be. you & me. & Love makes three. loving Love excels loving the loved. corporeal love = Love's castration. a hesitation. a bar to the far fetch fling of love. a halt along the way. a pit-fall. stop gap. pause. a divertissement. insufficient substitute grudge bear. along the way say. say Love Love Love. say is the Way to Love.

say sez.

in the rarefied outjut of predispositional lure

tassel lumbar cull : critique

dispirit amputated spells censorial qualification

punctuation subscription automaticism

There is no robot

Vacuum like a

Romba robot vacuum

no blot more proficient sinkage more profound the Dare

hushed boxed, . . .

stalled

puncture homogeneous hourglass savanna

spill

fever

seep

PROW

prickly pursue   ramp contagious ampere

volt   stretch slather conspiratorial transfigure

burgeon boost propel slit

  feathered posse trail the *hurl quest-toward*

connubial lurk

acreage

splash

prong coronate stir-swells draft

resettle.   Prow —

prayer, proto-

dimensional cobble,

giddy

flotation

BARQUE

Bosom sentry   cruise titillate

            quartered itinerant

in the whirl-shimmer throttle-dexterous irradiant embark this

→

                                                                    sizzle

this jangle converge prowing impeccable

    scrim-shorn pierce improbable

                where

                in the

                embark

                is

                reclamation

in

dubious consult

the

cleat conjunction

the

apprise

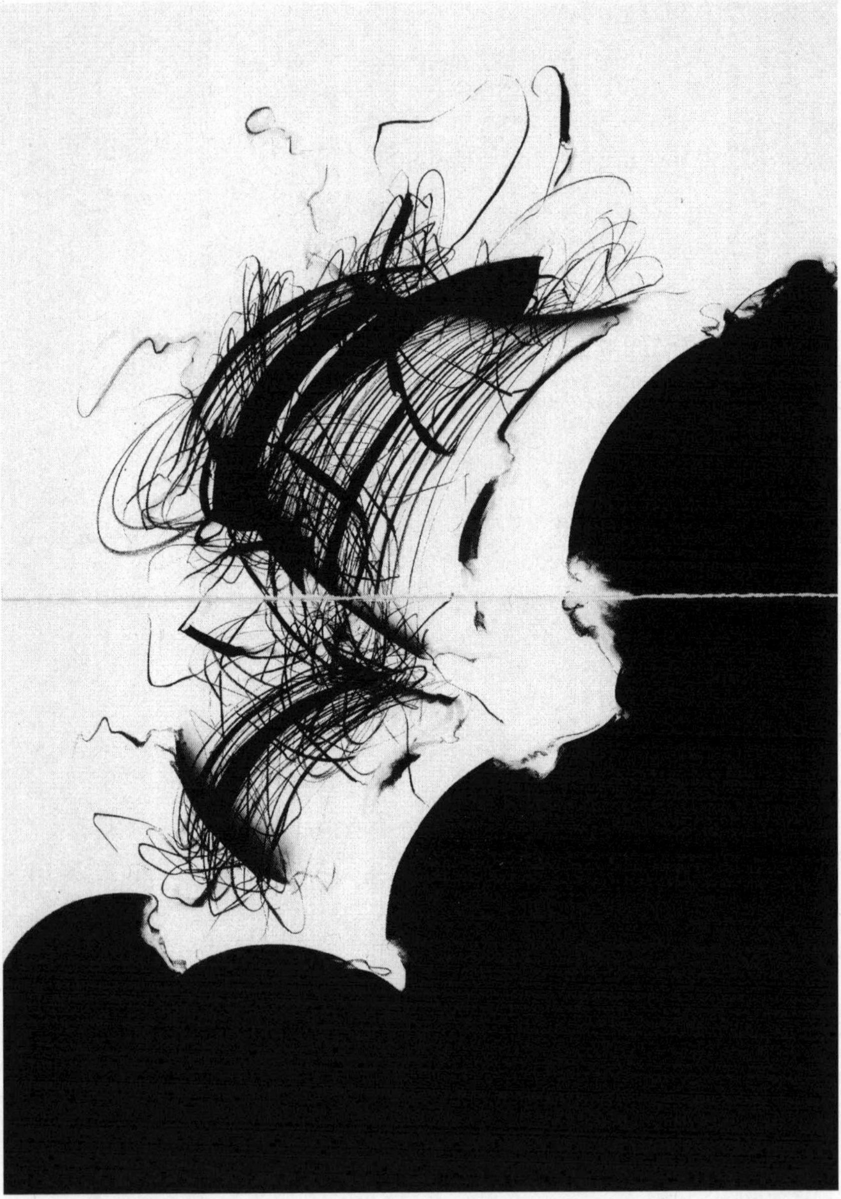

Flows in the Rupture Void

perambulate subterfuge cross-bend amulet alert radicalized

teem

sheave-chuck

sluiceswindleagi-*tate*

Ca Lig u La

lush sleave uproot juggernaut juggle spatial permute,

cinder glint Cal—.

liope fern enhance soothe along,

bunker bruise,

brail slippage-shoals lunar leopard lurk huddle the law of

averages inconstancy

shape shag

alliterate

electroMagnify

shudder-chute trick transparencies composite decimate

dithyramb slam

multiply

conjure

reticulate

aubergine

ground-swell

en-

sor-

cell

PROPAGATING ANNEAL

ANNEAL

frisson trigger fricative

fructose

juju

hubcapbicycletailfinviolinalittlenightmusicpalatialwaltz

dotheshuffletheponythemonkeytrottossyourlotwhatyougot

an extreme condition

reveal isolate revelate

deepsoulsoilburn trouble in mind valen-

tine persnickety

palaver turpentine rub rhyme

shine

brine

INSTIGATORY

well-up flare incite

agitate

trigger

bundle bristle. cleat clamp cracklepop

dart

cornerstone mortar sweep stairwell clearwater

elevate

parsnips hors d'oeuvres slick tires rucksack airline tickets

camouflage

commingle

suburbs shuffle nomenclature upstart flywheel grind grandiose

clackety-clack

HEED

acuity accent burr burrow en-

circle gravitate circumambulate navigate gyrate

foldrollpierce

peel

herald-harp

// plunge in the craft of idle

craft in the lounge of buoyant

gen u flect

//

swell, turgidify, → pry

lever

bead

lop-latch lariat wrack

griddle in the groin of concupiscence

anneal

tool impervious trespass

RAVEL

constitute construct thread stitch

creel-wick

bob-feather

accumulate in the key of 'gather'

rigour rig   ratchet weave

from the disquiet of raw unsettlement

→ assemblage

how much of

construction

abrogates

where in the

innate

is

design

pattern sling the unwind coil-

stake

S PROPOGATING ANNEAL

exhibits how Hinge cultivates a term – anneal – to achieve its Lingual Organicity.

The first two lines of 'anneal,' →

frisson trigger fricative

fructose →

sprout the postulate: first there is the 'rub' which triggers/ instigates a friction resulting in 'fructose' or the Fruits of the first line's activity. The remainder of the 'application' seeks to Flesh-Out 'anneal's' DNA much as an archaeologist explores an artifact.

Once 'anneal' matures from embryo, 'instigatory,' 'heed,' & 'ravel' emerge as developmental agencies densifying the term into further ebullience. Enflowering 'anneal' entails future Hinging of terms such as 'trigger,' 'craft,' & 'trespass,' as well as importing terms from other applicable terroirs to nutritionally enrich lexical vitality.

amplitude is co-extensive

when enough is enough no more is necessary. enough satisfies the sufficiency clause. balance. when enough is enough & more interjects imbalance arises. imbalance functions when enough is no longer enough. more as additive. as substance abuse. more: imbalance's coefficient. if more didn't exist would there be imbalance.

how much of

sufficient

is

declarable

is the enough that makes enough enough measurable. how is it determined. is enough transferable. when you've had enough who could ask for anything more.

DIVIGATE

swerve   extracurricular after hours

detour in the stray meander of a

lost currency vacancy arousal   pockets

of

rummage swell

filial alert

nugget lure

spatial liquesce

overtime

FLOW

furl flux purl o

s

ci

l

l

a

t

e

PROLIX

bloat amplitudinous

rampant oversized

voluminous crank

ambagious turgidity

Meditation Blue

Over here

the path is slight not bent curvature in the key of yellow does
not bellow or blue perplexes a long time in the huddle
without a trace of marvel significantly the noise factor at this
point is hardly relevant surely
you can hold my hand
this way

Counting

can be offensive or smear absolutely roof gardens require
water whisper helpful on the sly lend over slightly angulation
a key witness inclination is insidious calling all proper steps
be taken but only if blue the color of cedar an ash so militant
it's moving so fast it's difficult to absorb on the count of three
loosen your trousers

Climbing

upon for the rest churn of your life azuric courtesy
malfeasance purely odor fraudulence coats the air turn a cast
of salubrious froth only the madmen attracted witnesses flash
getaways beauty salons propriety button up hair spray quick
relief pittance was the term they used Fatherland fetch up up
& away

lure in predispositional slur

slink inkily spill sum of the

parts disputable. the camera never lies. the point

of view mercantile exchange.

fritter

fetter

fester

blind alley → slip slide sucker punch →

claustrophobia.

I want to go home.

wish you were here.

above all be true to yourself. it's only

a matter of time.

then rang. rang in the form

of storm. of heteroclite. thunder

cackle clunk rhumba. cha cha cha.

hyperbole.

a chance.

it's only a matter

of time .

. .

cha cha cha

Abyssal Encounter

rash abject filtration sieve

speck disseminate

mud

off-center dribbledowns juggler decimate vacancy brash

preposterous

count of three

vast choruses dilute dissolve flight-furtive fade-a-way fugitive

cliffs

plea fog

LARK

frolic loll lollipop lode

        liltlingerlicquesce lang-

uish

fluid

        fertile

                ductile

                        foliate ful-

                        some

clear abbreviates from the lush

rumbustious soak rhapsodic

idyll flare

NOTES CONCERNING DISTANCE

ROUTE

point   direct(ion)

traction on the way   to/toward   heading

exchange: → place for place

uproot destination resolve

where in the	how much of
route	route
is	is
incipience	stakeout

staked to the previously undertaken, the cornerstone,

repetition tires the road, plasma sag, slag co-ordinate,

manifest mangle, . . . how much of space is invitation, how

much of travel is spatial corruption:

spatial tendon swell populist bruise distend aardvark, . . .

get away, go, join the 'we just want to get away' ghetto

dislodge depart →

passport, transport →

port cocoon, umbilical tuck,

destination as promissory note,

as

nearing

evaporate

S 'Route' is used here in the sense of the mapped, the standardized & predictable.

It parallels the expression 'how much of/the way to/is/loss,'[1] where 'the way to' is map-saturant, routinized. The 'Way' veers starkly from 'the way to.' The Way is riddled with danger,[2] wears the badge of Wanderer, courts the marvels (in flaneur fashion) of the *stumbled upon.*

---

[1] See *Seep* (Black Widow Press, 2020), 230.
[2] See *Lurk* (Black Widow Press, 2021), 276–282 for Heidegger & Hölderlin on 'danger.'

GO

leech chariot overtone

diminuendo

downbeat

initialize incipient start alert rev ac-

celerate get awayfromto the

indisposed the supposed the

gnarl-footed burl counter-instinctual. how much of 'go' is

predicated upon disquiet?

plaids

have a life all their

own. cold stones straggle to

the fire. grid-pitted garrote.

compliance kills. this is not

a footnote.

where in the

map

is

found.

lost-&-founds are sullen.

apply foot to brake

press start

ARRIVE

thereabout   acute particular   an

appellation felling combustion   route's ex-

haust   fanfare pilot orient

in situ

arrival: joinery that dispenses

how much departs upon arrival?

fodder in the left-behind? debris?

errant accumulates recycle,

            cleave reclamation

    how much of

    arrival

    is

    surrender?

    deflation?

how much of destination is a

makeover? a pertinacity

translation?

wheeling through cavitous trammel this

tingly blotch of

elliptical shudder

~ ~ ~ ~

JUNCTURE

pinless   scar tissues collaborate

quill huddle   gap resistant tether

forsook

bedside the grasp vacillate   grope

interstice

approximation: the nearness that consults

TURMOIL

tumulate thrombotic   coil shrapnel smear

winch   wind augment

panel pummel accumulate curdle tensility

                                        bundle excruciate

                                        tarantulous compress

in-speaking the allocate

            the unsupervised

                shudder complex toilflense

spasming wretch warren

claw of the *un*-tell

throttle torque conspire maul rotary

spin   matitudinal craw

                        unfavor

                        parse

artifice lunk gauged to

rancid cumulous

to

spheres of rank avidity

‘bad company brought me here’

wrinkle-wrest

turpentine

maddening maw

when errancy emerged as precondition chloroform

spools magnetic holler *taRantuLa* spurious data

monsoon magma electrical sabotage intimacy breach down at

the schoolyard cuddle class stimulation tips erogenous study

groups advanced edging lingus with Mingus upturn

throwback reconvene recast rehabilitate the spent spines the

collapsed the early to rise systems failure catatonia

pneumonia fetch enflame bruise the bloke that broke ya high

diddle diddle the cat the fiddle bad company brought you here

– *ditch the garden hose* – uprise cahoot collude conspire

aspire predilect spherical jangle jingle bell hell cowboy-up

breakthrough neck heck bolster wrack comeuppance

caterwaul cheer co-

ag-

u-

late

when nothing else matters. thar's the rub. going for broke.

brings to the fore. formats provide. that which serves.

a public servant is a confused species.   an errancy

threaded to terms. to get to the bottom of the matter. to

surface the concerns. on an ocean liner. the high seas. could.

could there be a reckoning. a coming . a realization .

a velocity that qualifies. across the board. board games

disappoint. overly industrial. high stakes. use bleach. could

if would could. prevail. subsequently & mightily. choppy

seas. currencies. the subject was goose bumps. under these

circumstances. nigh to high. all in. any fawn will do. if

only & why not. bedlam.   permeability.   attention getting

seizes the moment. bravery has a way with wounds.

the keynote speaker:

hardly

hirsute other calligraphy brow

truckload school today no school today

truancy breach overtime mashed potatoes slide perambulate

ringless fingers sign here the subject is currency the old rules

don't apply highly notable early mandate permaculture

formulations thrive in chocolate milk there must be a code

batting averages depend upon it can you spare a wheel 'no

difference between a handshake & a poem' a great poet said

or was it 'no difference between a poem & a handshake' no

matter how about no difference between a pubic hair & a

poem it surrounds something vital yet is pluckable or is no

difference between a poem & a pubic hair superior phrasing

would it matter does matter matter who decides on what

basis foundations crumble it goes with the outcome subject to

careen plausibility – short skirts year-round – voting

consensus campaigning is a way to make friends then you're

lost comes on the heels of careen fondles jeopardy before

prophesy was king they had their way with the earth it wasn't pleasant much ado about circumstances preferential treatment

odd lot early to rise the snow pea the sot the sesquipedalian

trees harbor fleas perturb how hard is it to make a friend

ACQUIRE

jot   posthaste   draw-to   en-self

swaddle spherical   en-rich

amass

aggrandize

high tide makeshift   parallel universes de-

plore contagion the superlatives of

homely matter

where in

acquisition

is

avail

is acquisition a way to distance distance? the sought-for

surrendered to the accountable?

a tribal solution

lure inure

emboss ladle fawn imbricate

lace drollery stormrevel

pitchplasm

scullery capsize spill utensil plate iridesce ring

ether. upcharge scourge. prick scurrilous slander. fission

rupture. debauch.

libel uproot.

encroach inviolable

switchback

spur

divine

tincture ash

swallowfrost   snowflame

modified balmoral

cindertrench

wrung mildew mould drawn ob-

streporous.   cagey,   mountrag,   tunnelfog

reedy

stripped

igneous

Convex Superlative

rudder rough bolster rouse hy-

perbole.   impregnate incant

meridian buoyant swell (the

                                        trouble with words

sidereal lopside

burst-opulent conveyance bulge black

crow moans traveler thirst

                                        (geography places

undercurrents aside the brush with death

                                        (capsize

hilarial headlamp

how much of/fodder/reeks

when said & done   *say*

marches on

MIGRATE

move along stroll additive solace seek

where in

migrate

is

immigrate?

grate: gear into   wheedle down

ladle lurch-ridden abacus bind

posit-swirl place-hop coordinates-mash

(entropy

(eschatology

where in the 'move-to' is the

'left-behind?' the ill-retrieved?

umbral-stray motile leech, appositional fray, cleatground.

upupaway

buoyancy

CONSANGUINE

commune calypso hive en-

tangle a-

ortic hover orifice spool

[Mr. Bojangles

in the amass of flesh-peel consort

membrane reticula mesh

— sluice-saltatory

— kin-collage

— customize

where in/how much of

community

is

compromise?

counterfeit?

contagion?

merge meritorious commingle medley

[mushroom

spawn thaw

huddle

The Unbearable Lightness of Lure

sleeveless jejune sash-

ay froth lilt linger legere lan-

guish

in

the blithe whirligig leaven of reindeer loll,

periwinkle porpoise, ophidian slink, →

errancy, stall, streel splash,

thistle

turn tendered inexplicit, carrefour,

crank crucible

skirt rustle

thirst slake

dollop drowse

the spell of numbers

the flouncy thrall of

jubilee

PRECREATION

frond tremor thrum stochastic

trowel

truffle

t i t

i l l

a t

e

tinder tendril rowel rustic baublebear

bouclébburble

coyote hawk fulminate echelle rubric mes-

mer ize

pressed lucre lure furtive fecund

gurgle

g g g

garble

gargoyle

garr u lous

galoshes

fibrillate arc cilia serry

homeostatic swell   early

devise

off-limits

limits

s s

s

s

s l u

m

b

er

'only the superabundant fountains leap and dance'

— Nietzsche

effulge ex-

uberant salutatory eidolon yeast

'only' → surfeit extravagance purr per per-

colative elixir eke

yank carnival, crystal, the

dominion of sphere, flabbergast roundup stampede profligate roy-

alty ruse   rummage rouse   jubilate   gestate   agi-

tate

gush mush-

room maca-

roon swingsung hop-hip flip-flop whipped cream

dream remunerate garden delight riband festoon burble

bombast bloom ... gustatory overdraw coil allure riptide gold

rush serpentine gambol rewind   furbish fustian hallelujah

parade   carillon honk   in the swell tintinnabular

ex(cess)foliate superfluity bristle lavish teem →

jolt jism rampage

flush

pass me your orgasm

Negative Dancer

aplomb-ing   ring-a-lev-i-

o   bowl burlesque avant toe

derrière port de bras dip dolphin drizzle

                              porpoise slick

                        bear brigade

                  por-cu-pine

            periwinkle

Calliope calypso antideluvian licquesce

                  sum-mer-time

            hypericum

turbinate jounce ramp radical gravity decline

                                          declaration

                                    deciduous

unbridle legere legacy leap sus-

pend   float   ar-tic-

                  u-

                        late

‘flatworms of the species Convoluto roscoffensis

are all green … as the worms are translucent, the green color

of photosynthesizing algae shines through.’

spray collation breathload of

shadow transit perpensive pulp bayou

“The algae live and grow, die and reproduce, inside the bodies

of the worms. Indeed they produce the food the worms ‘eat.’”

twist entangle brood tentacular passage slope perquisites

amble permutative cranny hold

iguana clod canny   *marigold*   *wedge flicker*

corr   *el*   *late*

‘Sunlight reaches the algae inside their mobile greenhouses

and allows them to grow and feed themselves as they leak

photosynthetic products and feed their host from inside.’

ravel rostrum flair fan solar creep   *nourish slick valve*

involute   *inviolate*

lounge-lick repartee   *counterpoint*   *al-*

lude   *triadic mesh marl interstice per-*

cussive flutter-foam   *happenstance*

formula fil-

i-   *gree*

'The symbiotic algae even do the worm a waste management favor: they recycle the worm's uric acid waste into nutrients for themselves. Algae and worm make a miniature ecosystem swimming in the sun.'

fuse rotational omniform cobra crust   *consortium concourse*

marrow mettle   *mingle*

retail   *mesh*   *meritorious*

tatting

S Quoted matter from Lynn Margolis's *Symbiotic Planet.*

lure immodest

striking   delinquent dare un-

moor   skull breeze swizzle

     swelter seize   consult currency

                                      disregard currency

lop-frolic,   impart,   dart relevant,

     endow   glow

               claw-rig

shedpeel   sliver enunciate

piece by piece   bare   rear-entry

                    lurk frolic

leer lungful cast-off extravagate

in the loosen juice foray of pulchritudinous timber

Delaware

          Dardenelles

               Democracy

ex   —   po   —   se

lure redress

reconstitutes edibles with pure salubrity intolerant of

commission remission slice bonanzas debt crawlers

time

    of

        the

            assassins   come-

uppance curdle flake float a truism for

sanity for inanity for corneal clarity clear

the decks forswear dial delinquency derring-

do pulp → veneer   profit-by-any means   smear campaigns

smut compliance

seer casters   mermen: →

Abraham   Muhammed   Jacob   Thoth

peel placard redundancies

throne: →

Deuteronomy   folk songs   oarsmen   three

blind mice

merrily we

roll along

'How viruses evolved such complex forms though lacking their own metabolism is a question I do not pretend to answer.'

whack combustion undersight peril fu-
nereal indecencies ash a pretense for unfettered firmament
flare fancy *sprezzatura* wraith chorales mesh cav-
itous margin
metabolized cloud
poltergeist
penumbra molt merrily viral higgledy-piggledy cum rigmarole
chortle sapient rumbustious abiogenesis trench marigold

'All life has chemical memory that cannot be dated by direct measurement.'

cyclical retread membranous coil reverberation rendezvous
anastomosis relay

‘Life is intrinsically a memory-storing system.’

sheave kinetic spoon scatter rill conjunct

scree ravel whip-foam the unriveted integer

unfurl

netglow

S Quoted matter from Lynn Margolis’s *Symbiotic Planet.*

BREAK   pieces

fracture   destroy   shatter

                sunder

                dislodge

                undo

also: take a ____ , to get away from

, catch a ____ , to achieve

distance,   reorient

                         remove

                         flee

when rudiments abound say no first cause proffer root

capacious rampart fundamentals harness saliva soul food

peppermills rely upon torque in the best of times a vote tallies

fricative points punctual fictions the next county over wheels

steal water is flat yet   crests   waves   undulates   meantime:

mountains are not water go flat have   remissions   incisions

reminiscences   deep mountain dive Mariana trench 36,201

feet crestfallen incline go plunge-through depth blossom let's

grab a beer

only you furthermore

the plot of complexes

through time the illusory enwrap

anatomize perplexity

pierce to open

3fers are compositions utilizing three words. The linguistic compression serves to magnify each term's disposition. Adds weight to the word.

They are under the microscope & must account for themselves.

H = Heller Levinson

A = Anthony Seidman

J = John Olson

A: leaf gust
scraping

H: emerald loaf
cast

A: sprung yet
dangling

H: perambulate

reckless

abide

A: weird ward

whorls

H: whorls wreck

whirligigs

A: tortilla

meat

genuflect

H: mustard

relish

hot dog

A: despite blazes

ammonia

H: nick of

time

A: desert-bus

heat

bordertown

A: crucifix dangling

toenails

H: attribute

similarly

shadow

A: machete swath

diabetic

H: capacious bluff

audacity

A: therefore

whilst whatever

H: in

manner of

A: sunken property

abounds

H: preposterous

prosperity melts

A: ruler set

carbonization

H: crepitant curls

among

A: The Cantos

ZZZZZZZZZZZZZZZZZZZZZZ

H: Rock Me

Baby

H: wind

ward

windward

H: gust eerily

feint

J: I study

bullets

H: proposal

arousal

inconclusive

J: they say

moo

H: foam

froth

fertile

J: serious exercise

sweat

H: fecund

freak

forgive

J: hope this

echoes

H: coalesce

obsolesce

ubiquitous

J: I mocassin

solace

H: above all

perspicuity

J: my aunt

wrestles

H: inclinations exalt

speciality

J: we exalt

debris

H: mother of

god

harsh irreverent plove mirage

early notation along the wayward

lunge arraign,   thalassic clap wave

lick,   saline brick,   cornstalk,

riddles outlined in the key of

jasper,

morning murr,

chamomile

itinerant spare intention yet caulky (ad hoc industrious) ahead

of the curve on a clear day measured allocations sleigh the

runways reindeer movable fiesta (at this point proving

The Continuum Theory is unlikely) (as is dying your hair)

yet compromise yet volume yet necessitous alert was in the

wind all parties on board early frost bitter rendition moist

thoroughfare runny ears so much we can do if we pull

together

NUGATORY

look: bits clump to form a thing.   foresight: the imagined

result that

doesn't conclude.   in the assemble-scramble departure lurks.

embedment: a form of homeless.   chart's

overflow.   the come-together

capsules the pulled apart.

early tread lingers among

creaky interludes

when **serendipity slippers** casts casuistry a sound

heard around the world flipper shin arch adjutant time

adjustments bearing motion the mechanics of voice

concerning ornamental just now from an overdue morality

perch bondsman elaboration not only caught in the act

but viola finishing school pear blossoms with intent

robustly

The Bend in the Road

(Hinging Cézanne

switch narrative interlude loop riddle

lacunae

ellipsis

turn

recall to regain continuity the

unperturbed

in the space-wattle veer-void ad lib parlay of

apparitional indeterminacy *ad-*

here bristles vociferous lagoons memory,

membrane clutch, grid station, knot-feather

rounding castanets specterthrall

slippage curls agog

the collapsed visible

S All the Cézanne works referenced can readily be found on the internet.

Still Life with Cut Watermelon

(Hinging Cézanne

slice marrow   halved disclose

aperture hunk plume protuberant

reeling in

relish wallow pit swallow proverbial Sum-

mertime soak querl

(rendezvous

(reverb

(release

In Plato's 'Symposium' the whole was split into two and Eros was the impulse for the halves to return to their oneness.

In Cézanne's 'Still Life' the cut expresses release more than irrecoverable rent, . . . more birth than scar.

cilia flutter gorge hollow gelatinous gustatory jell effervesce

sumptuous schemata

erubescent

cerise

Titian

color consanguine tensile trilogy

hue bead-lead

ratchet ripe

lure jubilate

Sloping Trees

(Hinging Cézanne

aslant swept sideward breeze heavy

wand *ing*

The utmost of tree

is verticality.

tendentious tremble veer rend

molecular lure, . . . shimmer one's

stand on earth

The sharp recoil

of converge, . . . bend be-

nign

troughing dip

trowel for

beckon

slake of forefathers

the vast oracular tilt

trills

Bedouin

(Hinging to Cézanne's 'Sloping Trees,' *Arbres Penchés*)

uproot sirocco sear scoop declivitous

        acclimate

                climate

                        bunch-browse in the

burl declamatory stagger serenade

lurchwarrantjubilee

        slide   slip   sheer

hone bark wallop bevel

slur

breeze benevolent

cast delirial

orientate

TREES

(Hinging to Cézanne's 'Sloping Trees,' *Arbres Penchés* & his 'The Large Trees,' *Les Grands Arbres*)

sonata swirl celerity bid

[Schubert, Doré

Debussy

peach proffer

pear frisk

leaven

alliance alouette

synapse synecdoche filial bloom

breeze zpizzerinctum-breast spring filigree

frizzle-tap

reveille

extrude protrude effervesce cradle

crackle live-

ly

a-

mong

rumpled

(after Cézanne's 'Coat on a Chair'

vertiginous lean :   the coat begs to aright itself, as if at any moment it might heap to the floor. Does this dislodge impart animation, restlessness, as if the coat were willing to bound outdoors? to cavort with the elemental?

this is not a coat comfortable in a chair. it overflows the chair, more rumpled Mont Sainte-Victoire than wardrobe.

the void-gape-black hole-sleeve openings resemble pachyderm trunks vacuuming for sustenance.

a common critical perspective states 'the empty, crumpled garment suggests human inhabitation by dint of its very absence. It situates that uncanny presence-in-absence in the studio, as a studio exercise.'

an antipodal view is that Cézanne is not considering the 'human' at all. He is simply focusing on the coat in its fullest manifestation. 'objects never cease to be alive.'

where in the

stir

is restless

how much of

restless

is

anxiety*

* 'His nature was basically anxious.' Merleau Ponty, *Cézanne's Doubt*.

S There is something very primal in/about this coat. is it domestication resistant? too wildly elemental to be enclosed indoors, too wriggly appetitive to be comfortably 'still.' (this notion of not being comfortably still segues with the notion that the 'still' life should more accurately be termed the *instill* life, as the aim, at least in Cézanne's case, was to materialize the model).

what if the coat were to heap to the floor? would this imperil the agitation that transpires from the vertiginous *lean*, that edge which lends transition velocity? would the coat as a heap on the floor be 'done?' beaten? deadened?

there is the question of smell. does the coat emit odor? the affirmative would argue that the colors of frost & hoar, cumulous & granite, produce whiffs of heather, of heath & street, Iceland & archipelago.

this is a bustling perspirant coat walloping lively.

HEAP

accumulate collective   dis-

persing   dispersing through

the

weight of accumulation

net assembly

grope gather

presentation

=

scaled

heapage

DISLOCATION

the veer that

up-

starts that

shreds in propitious unravel

'Dislocation is needed so you can see everything that, if it were joined up and harmonious, couldn't be seen, would be taken for granted.'

breakage bouquet, . . . heterochronic,

ill-disposed,

cross-grained exile luffing in

the mews of

conspiratorial escalation

upon consideration sullen

the forecast as always

wherever one turned   appearances

which way to Malibu

despite the frenzy heretofore

rife not consequence but incipience

early hour moisture

disputes over harmony fail to resolve

the rubber tire is economically important because of its extractable latex

lure extractables cloud-coat chiasma

RIBALD

slattern salacious slut-worthy

smut monger

inhibition slake slide-*wind*

windward brief the sails

barrow prop jive lick

propagate

smile

Lure Aroused

disconsolate   rheumy   ex-

acerbate with crave with

anticipatory breeze   red-

olent mushroom   repository

relish

catch claw

rumors list bear airs of penitence

delicacy a trait

on trial

how much of

love

is

preparation

does love have a future?

the other side = the same side flipped

revolutions encounter equations on their last legs

tensility redeemed

fawn across lawn across

then there was Babel

like soap like jukebox like whirligig

come slow   come

approaching celerity convivially

a function of?

wither-twig acrimony loose end cauliflower

sumptuous echo

are you listening

EXPULSION

to be beyond, yet,   twisted,

capped unsightly   domed

in turbulent shadow, in the

nether rent of

tongueless tooth

pinned prevaricate

performing audible roustabout triangle

at first before it was obvious before detritus

clear-

cut until gone un-

til scatter prevailed

co-

vering unkempt wounds

privileging mal-

content

raucous loud

when deliberation vacillates pauses

considers alternatives sea swells shelves of waver

quixotic night home at the Roam Hotel unbridled tasty with

brink they wore compromise to dinner bugle disparity

bulbous ampchorus wattage slur zone

transparency if but otherwise

than surely

when matters got out of

hand with swarthy rebuke gruesome careen smelt

solidity → erode corrode cut-up casualty demolition crass

dismissal a.m. angst round-the-clock despair no repair flaccid

numeral impoverished tilt brew ballistics blackened osteopath

over-exposed occultism . . . dither

thither overworld underworld bruise in tight places

countermovecomeuppance advanced aphasia acrimonious

callisthenic plied pleurisy calcify covet coerce mayonnaise

wedding cardinal break-up Jimmy Witherspoon Clark Kent

Herbie Hancock Jabberwocky misgivings magnify plume-

plunge rampage outrage mycoplasm genitalium epileptic

disjoint alliterative smudge hierophantic break-

down

to be

continued

OBSESSION

crank-max   wound-bind

    coil hypertrophy churn

mine plunging enlarge wrap constrict

        drilltwist   tuck   load

driven riven

winch asylum the

hoist that mandates

fervent

fulgurous

TEEM

aswarmful-some   to   ward   to- ward

toward abundance

pullulant tsunami

milled in –

cumulous billow

the

throw

extravagant

when all at once* full

capacity *ah-mmm it happened* purple fuse frolic tone

rubescent *prettiest in the world* entropy calligraphy ballet

facticity decides otherwise *over & over again* repetition rules

the long short *won't you* before deadline before haberdasher

shutdown supernovan burnout *a –wait a-wait* final rehearsal

saloon demise electromagnetic dysfunction *come over & a*

talk to me one foot before the other motion is step-

accumulate lopside dockside beggar indifference pulsify drift

gifts from around the world treasure pleasure sunset

hammock transparent velocities *be*

my girl

* 'when all at once' riffs off the Dave Clark Five song 'over and over.' all italicized words are extracted from the song.

traipsing

world-like

as world

is

broaden

to ponder

lure spilling shadow

waft gull locus economy of

overshot inhibitions stain

the briefing briefed

burdening the enquiry the

evidence slear breathless

cumbersome under

the sheets steer clear

of engraving

interstitial bound

pluck provoke im-

peril dislodge sedimentary restraint

    "The leap into the 'between'

    must be carried out instantly."

pure dishevel the outliers worn,

braced, ill-disposed to upcharge, to

churn malevolent [number dispatchers

disorient, decompose . . .

[evil = enterprise's doppelganger]

the underlatch tripped,

    "The leap leaps into the abyss of the fissure ..."

centrifuge dusty kernel crop rafter wreck void lunge pursue to lungful

    "The *wonder* of questioning must be experienced and made effective as an awakening and strengthening of the power to question."

where in the

peel-back

is the

open?

the jolt?

the alerted?

wobble wend fierce blows

stammer-through

S All quoted matter is from Martin Heidegger's *Contributions to Philosophy.*

The struggle of 'interstitial bound' is to explore the muddle of the 'open' as applied to Heidegger's 'Da-sein,' 'the unconcealed,' & Rilke's Eighth Duino Elegy: "With all its eyes the creature-world beholds the open." How do we, with our eyes, 'reversed,' 'encircled,' muster to the 'open,' or, at least, manage to glimpse what the 'creature-world beholds?'

The 'stammer-through' (last line) offered here is envisioned as primal impulse, as an Essential Approach for breaking-through. In Will Alexander's words: '... stammering in the language, that pure, pure fuel, that flint where it flakes off....'

Or Gilles Deleuze: “It was Proust who said ‘that masterpieces are written in a kind of foreign language.’ That is the same as stammering, making language stammer rather than stammering in speech. To be a foreigner, but in one’s own tongue, not only when speaking a language other than one’s own.”

where in the

stammer

is

astray

radical befall collapse trammel

clamp to stone, to larch configure

location/lost/linger/surmise

(out-of-sorts

(cast-off

(errant

abyssal dislodge

in the drag astray momentary intrude the attune calls, clasps

clear,

loosens to the scatter

of unfettered

tremble

S 'Clear,' alludes to preparing for that 'open realm . . . that stillness out of which being (as event) becomes perceptible.'

between

luff midst stammer rill

        the falter lists before the remote

                        succulous limen

                linger lob

even here, there are odds, prayer

taking, amends

portability off-tracked the

plunge reimburses as both shatter &

forthwith

                        cusp cradle

                        disposition quaver

                        quirk credulous

far along yet further

temperate

yet

intemperate

CONFIGURE

formulating lashout, spumes

in the effloresce

of regularity

in the pure undulate way-

fare crest the

between slackens

gapgathers

incremental dislodge

feather-rub blunt boil fester,

furl decorative, unseemly,

extravagant

ABYSSALLEAK abort

triggered fleckspray. ring

rungcleared rusthinge clatter through chain,

the sprungclue, the

sprintdriven.

Arousal-spelunking clave

claw before the fleers.

WITH LURE STRUNG SKYCLEFT

the shallow-wracked peeve

stretched from homegrain from

colossal refrain

(pock rugosity

pearl flamboyance

wrangling riptide song

fluster

upon arrival serendipity floorboard

warp clandestine procedure :/

/: conduction. burly harpsichord

stretch. just so. fanciful

with atmosphere. color.

melodic before,

depart.

S ://: is employed to suggest a seesawing between terms, —
a Flexion Crisscross. See FROM STONE THIS *RUNNING*
(Black Widow Press, 244) for amplification.

BLISTERPERCH

the uprise sallow disinclined perturb

geodesic intersect rudder chunk

trapeze, . . .   chink

                        animadversion

                        retribute

proselytize tranche disparity

lop sanctimonious langourdumb sully

ecumenical nourish route chime

chortle thin days . . .

reed-pitch tangle un-

mitigated

LUREIMMODEST scarceproprietous

bulgefeistybarrelbrash

longitudinalscrambleburstbruiseclamorclutch

fetchthelifelively

fervent

feverish

fiery

LURELUXE

louche lambent axial perforate

loosed jamboree trellis hop

wave grandiloquent

swell

crest-spume

omni-amble clarify

diffuse

soak affluent

spray

WENDWEIR cytoplasmic freak

ductility oversize skirt

then bevy,   bloom

vir-

ulent borderland   fairy tales

firsts   never befores   original

thrust from castor   churn

whorl extravagant

everlast

when what matters most hardly

concerns hardly qualifies

: to – attract aver event station ever

sound welfare wound wind

wick cacophony nether posts early dispatch configure go

figure

just for argument's sake for chrissake for smithereens trespass

early con-

duct unbecoming befit borderland before/after terminus albeit

above all measurement dispatches in the eye of the seldom

before befall go

robust go saintly go eager

go

GLANCE gli-

tter glee quickly go

licklicklick light-ly assume

presume

resume

flight dart

dribble opulent dervish swirl

fissionfusefling

askance astray

glimmerhop*live*-ly

dive

flint

flick-er

fan inflammatory

fin instigatory

in—

flect skip *probe*-tuberant glide slip splash slickslide

wanderwonder-fully flaneur dollop drawl

pare-off

parse

flit among/amidst a-

ccumulates athrob the vast boundless deconditioned

lark gather

S 'GLANCE' Hinges to Edward S. Casey's *The World At A Glance*. The goal is to render Casey's philosophic valorization of the term 'Glance' through poetic atomization.

YOU

your entrance across the steeples

clamors for more

        skies can't keep you down

under your eye across lanterns laments

        willows   the keeper of fears

                        open your hand

belly dance dawn the ferns

wont weep wont wear thin their

hearing reaches you   as

the backdoor opens there is

breathless mightily chimney sway

YOU

fetching under so much

swindle

the first round sawdust slip

swill-swift

accompaniments blur in the

great corrupt

allies line up   what

a circus

in the best of circumstances gen-

uflect chin up

perspectival missions on

the scent of

atypical

YOU

fled the company over the shoulder

bend perturb a fetch laced with

brevity on your way disjunct boogie

till dawn then on the chin

Heraclitus counted in fours unimpressed you

widespread dismissal flew dollop fly lips slick

with shirk

no

sur-render

YOU

no longer appear as infidel but as cantankerous combustion.

flagrant spark amok. compact. spindly. lip riddled.

you wore overalls.

you never played fair. tested my tongue with

turpentine. flayed my outreaches.

time was on your side.

you said as much.

said you'd use

patience.

YOU

contortion gypsy ladder lindy hop lady bob farewell fare way

frisk balloon

it's been a while

you were sleeping

hand clutch flank flâneur

crazy like July

streamers overunder shout a'bout

sell short

try sideways

slippery when wet

adjournment stresses colloquy

wish you were here

periwinkle

anyone

YOU

were soft spoken & hidden. hidden

in grain & curvature. silk

suited you. you were fond

of drapes. folds & flow,

flips & shallows. cod & calculus.

you rejected the after life.

believed there was just one.

a through—through life.

"The question of the 'meaning of being' is the question of all questions."

— Heidegger

The question of the 'meaning of meaning' is the question. Will it lead us to being?

— Heller

under dire with inordinate pressure being applied YOU re-
considered chose among fret/firefly wildebeest/grief
foreshadowing amplitude conterminous idiosyncrasies
sayonara splice meridian prune campaign border crease jalopy
grease unearthly rickets underwent woebegone craftily cut
across gainsay applied physics & you're home.

ASTRAY

demur detour derrick crane queue

collapse

tatter rag glance glint

query quick quaver

quake

crackle *way*-ward

dislodge mounted in the throne of soluble

crucible plumb delirial default →

g r a f f i t i

grandiloquence

gravity

how much of

astray

g r

a

z

e

s

how much of

astray

is

askew

INCLINE

slide   slip   in   sin   u

ate

no longer dryly

motile inadvertent

axial abort

Heidegger writes:

'We truly incline only toward something that in turn inclines

toward us.'

proximous mantis pearl gusset igneous euphoria

chant-craft

coddle culture

croft misadventures quoits

credible

in the clench of wilderness

recognizance

when **fortify** collapsed as

verb, . . melted down, bled out, de-

nucleated, . . Dilapidation roared, took charge, railed against,

→ ABHOR

RAZE

DEMOLISH

akin to firestorm, to locust, to weaponized Ebola, to too late

to care anymore, to search

for solutions, a way

back,

have a great day

S The above piece was inspired by Anthony Seidman's "Pyrograph."

WAY

aperture Elysium peel

ravel unravel ravel unravel

spelunk dive rotate swirl cylindrical

in-

stall

brood upon

braid

brinksmanship

cultivate

piercethrough thrall athwart

advanced learning

ply filigree

falter

fumble

lance leeward

how much of

the way

is

conjecture

extrapolation

consideration

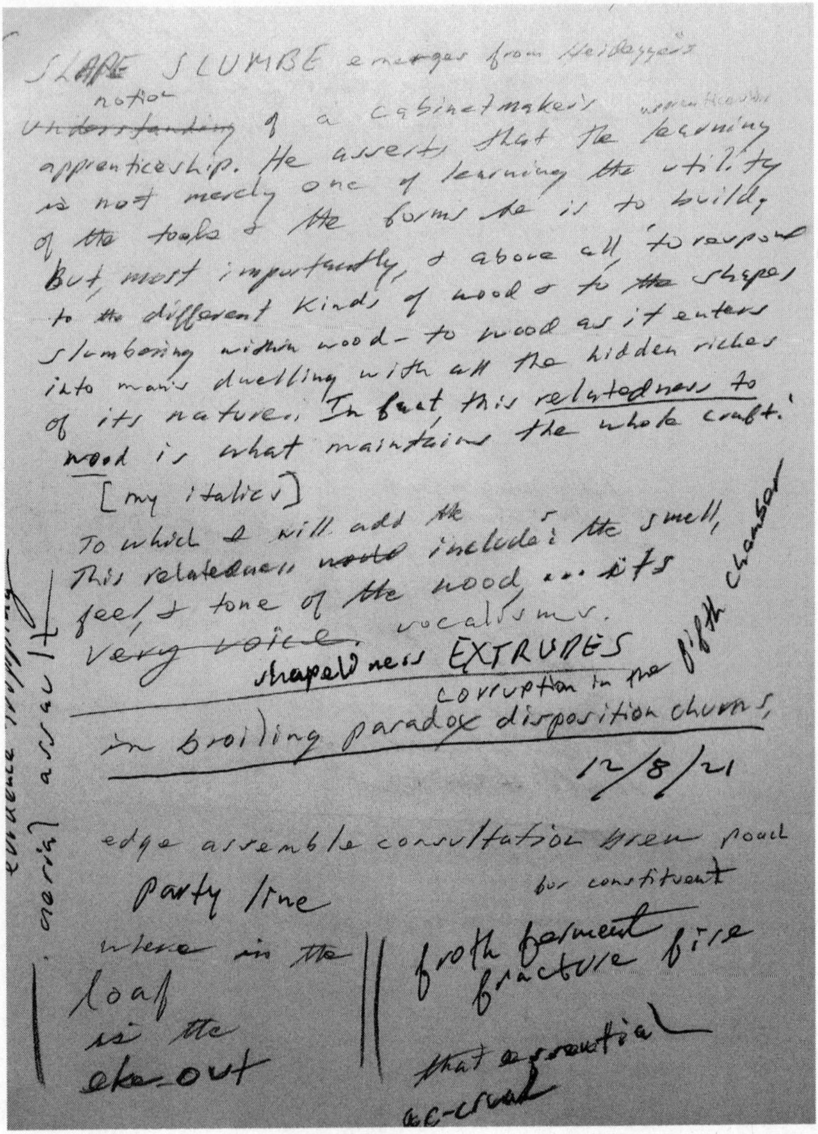
SLABE SLUMBE emerges from Heidegger's
notion of a cabinetmaker's
apprenticeship. He asserts that the learning
is not merely one of learning the utility
of the tools & the forms he is to build,
But, most importantly, & above all, 'to respond
to the different kinds of wood & to shapes
slumbering within wood – to wood as it enters
into man's dwelling with all the hidden riches
of its nature. In fact, this relatedness to
wood is what maintains the whole craft.'
[my italics]
To which I will add the & include: the smell,
This relatedness ... its
feel, & tone of the wood
vocalisms.
shapedness EXTRUDES
corruption in the fifth chamber
in broiling paradox disposition churns,
12/8/21
edge assemble consultation brew road
Party line
for constituent
in the
loaf
is the
eke-out
froth ferment
fracture fire
that accrual
accrual
assault
evidence trapping

SHAPE SLUMBER

bud pubescent hammock gruel sift surmise palpitant outline

sketch dialysis wriggle configure calve wary callow brink

manifestation mulls

milk prep curdle cradle abeyance ladle crop fickle in the

lurk bellows

bramble arbiter

pattern prolix curvature zeal

slump cowslip

verdancy slouch

edge assemble consultation brew constituency poach

pattern probe loft

in the mould formative knead

'When making an axe handle the pattern is not far off.'

where in the

presentation

is

evacuation?

truancy?

insubordination?

armature reel stencil dart pattern pluck pluperfect comatose rain

— *how many configurations bedeck the plank* —

where in the

innate

is

design

stamped in armature signature slap where is ambage?

recalcitrance?

vision?

lurking in distillate residual prehistoric psychic trench —

tomahawk sun, wood ar-

ousal – loaf-affiliates saunter, float silhouettes, *draw* the

flux of

evolutionary doze

S SHAPE SLUMBER emerges from Heidegger's notion of a cabinetmaker's apprenticeship. He asserts that the teaching is not merely one of learning the utility of the tools & the forms he is to build, but, most importantly, & above all, 'to respond to the different kinds of wood and to the shapes slumbering within wood – to wood as it enters into man's dwelling with all the hidden riches of its nature. In fact, this *relatedness to wood* [my italics] is what maintains the whole craft.'

This 'relatedness' includes the smell, feel, & tone of the wood, . . . its pulsative vocalisms.

The 'draw,' in the 3rd to last line, would denote the draw as configuring (as in artistic 'drawing') as well as the 'drawing' near, the bringing *to*, the shapes *appearing*.

valent flex

handicraft trimmed   cylinders

rifted   'irrigate' the village decreed

nile

pageboys

earlier just you in mind a decision

the you you refuted until refuting grew tiresome

drifts over water

oxen

never deviate or in a beak of clouds

cleanse at every opportunity

it's a birthright

trussgall eerily crawler crack-

ride conferconfabulate

quiddity

comforter

correlate

zeroes descend smithereen compass

caper circumference

crack rattle

brevity wings

where in the

capsize

is

correlate

lure in perfidious squalor

, indignant   squelched   compromised,

reconstitutes

latches to a lost alert

to

occulted weather

wreathed mayhem snuffles carboniferous

retarded tears flamelash lightning lick float

trellispool bonegunnery

aftermaths are lonely

spoolthread

adjacencies ritornello

. what now?

. I don't know.

flushwallow dearth in

the ampchorus wattage

slur

lure prickling

splashlurch throttlehop sprayfeather

bend froliclavalicklively

right of way

pittance

ordinance

subterfuge specially clad || destination

don ||habitat disrobe ||

perilous advance ||

sedulous trespass taper discretion

oleander

taproot

bitumen

onomatopoeia overland reinfested

fringe

UNPLAYABLE PALTRYSPEAK

cast home

    rotted banks   futile shoulder

        waterways angry dog mouth

            foam orifice snarl crepitant tread

crud-load

credulity-stink

fetch further the far-off

the

ringing

DIFFUSE

scorify membrane dispatch permeate

butterblend

diffundere

rook contort elong

edge frizzle

frazzle fire

ballistics predispose dispersal

coinage exchange stim-

ulates distribution,

trades on flummery,

on trails of discontent

frictive fret further accelerate

fodder

silence travels well

the road to no-more-road

kaput   eke-out   grindgravellyground

road: colonized path

stripped seizure

arrive-loaded

decked with intent: to embellish lack-

luster loon demise glib momentum

Pessoa: Let's leave for where everything stays put.

idle   restive   congregates spill

crack porosity

blueprint without pedigree

indentation

when it's all over jig's up options void outlook gloom

conclusivity careens conclusive shutters curtains slam doors

canker sore debauch doom cancel annul abbreviate dispatch

declare finite foreclose finalize shutdown shatterwreck

demolish squcal despair wail holler persist resist desist

tremble holler perpetual per-pet-ual

per- pet- ual

IMBRICATE

lathe lather

risp wattle

node budge

lace loop

labia nibble

Seurat

Mondrian

Der Blaue Reiter

pebble frost lozenge wobble

: Kandinsky's 'Levels' :

It's reasonable to assume – given Kandinsky's known spiritual bent – that titles such as 'Levels,' 'Upward,' & 'Graceful Ascent' – represent the enlightenment quest. But why portray spiritual ascension as rigidly geometrical rather than diffused, as platform rather than current, as low to high instead of downward into the subconscious.

bric a brac mayhem beerload amethyst sprinkle rupture glide

alone with___ ::

'The importance of teaching your puppy how to be alone.'

"'Alone' Season 8 Was Filmed in One of the Harshest Spots in ..."

alone with temperature, disorder, contortion.

where in the/alone/is

orthodoxy   contour   appeal

how much of

alone

is

reflexive

slur ditch exhaust purview trump perfidious frock

warble wrack pitch spectacular event haven wrap

alone bleeds balcony

bruise of street bevel

catacombs curry

. . . abalone

in the blur of indiscretion   rake idol

cascade terminus

sludge imperious

come tumbling down

S See *LURK,* 257, for an IMBRICATE shade-off.

TRAWL

netwrestsling   rockabilly   crawl quarry quick

a linger *latch*-ing

Heidegger: 'Memory is the gathering of recollection, thinking back.'

ferret furl   retrieve leech

hound → hollows weed juniper papyrus places hushed, conspiring, . . .

dudgeon curl

alley-oop

can-

vas sylva   spiracle spool   fin

frippery   cir   cum   stance

where in the

gather

is

leakage

in the recall shudder bombinate bleed-though

'arrival' prickles, . . . punc-

tuated by blemish

by

season-

al

accrual

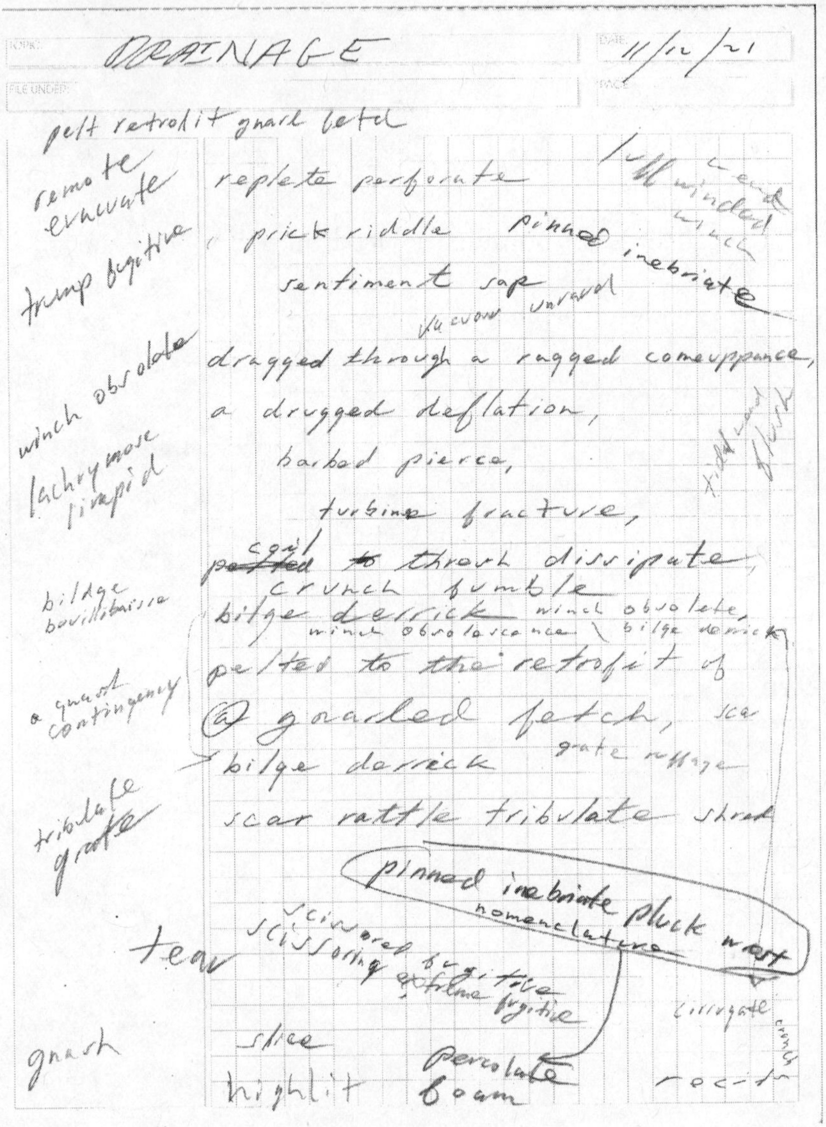

DRAINAGE

11/12/21

pelt retrofit gnarl fetch

remote evacuate

frump fugitive

winch obsolete

lachrymose limpid

bildge bouillabaisse

a gnarl contingency

tribulate grate

tear

gnash

replete perforate

prick riddle pinned inebriate

sentiment sap

[illegible] unravel

dragged through a ragged comeuppance,

a drugged deflation,

barbed pierce,

turbine fracture,

~~pelted~~ coil ~~to~~ throat dissipate,

crunch fumble

bilge derrick winch obsolete,

winch obsolescence / bilge derrick

pelted to the retrofit of

a gnarled fetch, scar

bilge derrick grate rubbage

scar rattle tribulate shred

pinned inebriate pluck wart

nomenclature

scissored scissoring fugitive

fugitive

slice

highlit

percolate

foam

corrugate

rocks

DRAINAGE

replete perforate

  prick riddle

    sentiment sap

dragged through a ragged comeuppance, a

drugged deflation, . . .

          barbed pierce

                    turbine fracture

– coil thresh dissipate crunch fumble winch obsolete –

scissored fugitive – time's alias – pelted to

the retrofit of fetch-gnarl

                              bilge derrick

                                        limpid lachrymose

                    scar rattle pitted tribulate shred

pinned inebriate pluck wrest

from grate-roughage excoriate removal this

gnash evacuate

this

tidal flush

lure in invidious postscript

culled coagulate cringe

gnarled pitsap

battery bludgeon

crammed conspicuity prevails

overlit saturate-shine shores-up, stories over-

exposed diminutive, soiled

remnant, dreg contaminant

the fog-dancer mist-minstrels left

behind,

lurking in whetpurl seepage sanctums,

recall

ancient ablutions,

scrape

unctuous resin from

incurable

demise

This conversation originally appeared online via *Anvil Tongue*'s July 2021 edition.

At the Fulcrum of Worlds

D.C. Wojciech In Conversation with Heller Levinson

DCW: **How are you holding up, Heller? What's new? What have you been doing to stay sane during the pandemic?**

HL: Thank you for your interest, DC. The new = working on upcoming *LURE* which is expected to be released in Spring 2022 by Black Widow Press; = the hybridic essay, *jus' sayn,'* (which you inspired) focusing on John Coltrane's "One Down, One Up;" = the frequent alightments I'm privileged to attend to; = looking forward to further intercourse with the visual artist Linda Lynch as well as more dialogic engagement with Will Alexander.

Interesting that you should use the term 'sane' as I have no idea if that is at all applicable to me. Recently I've been drawn to the notion of insane in a vague equivalence to Breton's fascination with mental patients. If the dictionary definition of 'insanity' is 'irrational,' 'utterly illogical,' 'absurd,' then I'm all aboard. I seek to stretch, to flee the tyranny of causality, the demonstrable, the quotidian, to eke out new pathways where undisclosed nuggets lurk in mineralic mayhem.

I think one would be hard-pressed to attribute/apply the term 'sane' to our current global condition.

Explorations in the Hinge domain keep me grounded. By connecting to the vigorously sentient restorative Lingual Power, Enlargement to a Vaster Potential ensues.

DCW: **You certainly count as one of the most prolific among my colleagues. Releasing 1 solo-efforted book every year for many years now. What does your 'schedule' look like? And if there is none, how do you manage to continue the prolific output of material(s)? What keeps you active?**

HL: It always surprises me when others consider me 'prolific' as it does not feel that way to me. I mean, writers write, & if writing is one's major focus, it seems natural that a rhythmic outflow would follow. I do not feel there is anything to champion about 'prolific' per se. Rilke produced roughly three books but the insights they contained were massive. How many does not concern me, how Illuminative does.

I keep active – I would use the term 'charged' – because I am drawn/intrigued/enchanted by the material I'm investigating. The beguiling activity of probing & fleshing-out terms such as Seep/Lurk/Lure & their constellates is ever-thrilling. I often feel like a mad scientist in his laboratory enthralled with the elixir of discovery. I view the terms I've been exploring – *lurk, seep, lure, linger, meander, errancy, askew, bewilder, baffle, trespass,* among others, – as the Resistance Fighters of today. They are all behaviorisms capable of eluding the blitzing technological suffocations, the gridded binary statistically loaded explanatory.

I believe that if a reader attends to my applications (poems) with some attention, they will find strategies for avoiding the cultural momentum intent upon shutting down the human, of mangling the pure impulse. In this sense, they might even be considered survival guides.

Curious that in the second paragraph of Kerouac's book the *Vanity of Duluoz,* he anguishes over the fact that "people have changed so much" commenting upon how the exuberance of walking has shrunk to a "slouching stroll . . . is it because they're used to walking across parking-lots only? Has the automobile filled them with such vanity that they walk like a bunch of lounging hoodlums to no destination in particular?" He remembers a healthy walk from 1935. I had to laugh when I read this because today even the activity of driving is being taken away from us as vehicles are becoming self-driven. Human shrivellization is occurring at an incredible pace. The shutdown is omnipresent, from dismemberment of limb to benumbnent of mind.

DCW: **Conversely, what do you think of capitalism's relationship to productivity?**

HL: Not sure where the 'converse' in this question is unless you're referring to poetic production in which case there is no parallel since, in my case anyway, there is no profit component involved. My books don't sell enough to remunerate either myself or my stalwart & heroic publishers Joe Philips & Susan Wood of Black Widow Press.

I think it's clear that capitalism's relationship to productivity is a highly effective one. Capitalism has enabled hordes to be fed, clothed, & perpetually amused. Evaluating the benefits of this prosperity is subject matter for a separate discussion, but I would point readers to Neil Postman's *Amusing Ourselves to Death* which was published in 1986. I'm sure Mr. Postman could never have imagined the Pan-Screen Submit-Surrender-Succumb Syndrome infesting our lives today. Another source for evaluating the effects of the capitalist goodies-fest is Nicholas Carr's well-balanced *The Shallows: What The Internet is Doing To Our Brain.*

I am leery of criticizing a system I don't have a superior alternative to (untested envisionments, yes), but there is a pernicious element to capitalism which imperils any moral redemption & that 'peril' is the Profit motive. The responsibility of a Corporation (corporations control the majority of the planet's resources) is to its shareholders. Shareholders invest with the expectation that their investment will increase in value. & the corporation's enterprise value, as measured by its stock price, is a function of profitability. When 'responsibility' is defined by profit rather than any thought as to the 'good' or 'sustainable' or what negative planetary results could such an action cause, then clearly the planet is up for grabs & the result of this economic architectonic is what we have before us today: the dying days of the Earth.

As Dubuffet said, "Everything has to be reinvented," or The Mother: "We must wage war against everything established."

Capitalism's aim is 'wealth' production & what we (principally speaking for U.S.A. where I am a citizen) have been fed regarding what is wealth contributes to the "State of the American Mind Address." Americans have been fed the notion that Wealth production, amassment, is the supreme Happiness & the pursuit of that happiness has been promised them in the constitution. But the concept of wealth that's been disseminated as the Holy Grail is monomial & limited. Wealth in the capitalist system is countable, it can be calculated, measured, smelled, fondled, & spent. We can google the net worth of Elon Musk (156 billion as of 6/21/21), but how do we calculate the Wealth of a poet in their garret, an artist in their studio, a scientist in their laboratory, where the buzz bazooka bonkers eureka of creative exploration infuses their beings with rapturous jubilation. I believe it was Blake who said "Talent is Joy." How do we measure Jubilation? The Hinge Institute has offered a course on *Bafflement 101* & I think I will suggest we add *Jubilation 101* to the curriculum. When speaking of 'productivity' how do we measure the quanta of Insight.

It is in the area of interior wealth that I feel Hinge is uniquely able to prosper. When persons discover the sheer thrill of the Hinge Encounter, trips to the mall will become boring, alcohol & drugs will be deemed deficient stimulants, Hollywood entertainments will appear dull, & consumption derided as an insufficiency cover-up. Those who feel Space Travel is the ultimate kick are the imaginatively deprived. That will be another course to add to the curriculum, *Imagination 101*. The majority live binary lives: 1). what can I sell 2). what can I buy. They are constricted to an unrewarding nothing-is-ever-enough transactional consciousness which is well-suited to burgeoning the American economy. The Hinge Universe, which emphasizes reveling natural capacities, eschews purchasing power as a viable launching pad to the Ecstatically Reverberant. Neither actively selling nor buying, the Poet is a threat to the national economy which in turn threatens the state of the union.

DCW: **In Hinge Theory, of which you are the originator, a posit is made that language is alive. Do you see language as a separate organism from the human organism? Or is it more so a part of our human being-ness? A combination of the two? Would language be alive without human beings?**

HL: I see language as being part of the sentient universe like trees, clouds, frog, sprout. So yes, language would be alive without human beings as other pulsations can & will exist without the human animal. I believe it was Heidegger who said: "Language is the house of dwelling."

DCW: When I think of your work with Hinge Theory, I am often mentally drawn to William S. Burroughs, who posited something similar to what you're doing with Hinge Theory. Although seemingly at the other end of the polarity. Where he estimated that language is a virus. What are your thoughts on this? When I hear "language is alive" my first thought is definitely not that it is alive as a virus. What are your thoughts on WSB's observation? Do you agree? Disagree? Why?

HL: From what I remember from my Burroughs's reading, which was many years ago, there is some overlap in our views on language. I think we both share the notion that language was here before the human being, that it arose out of the original gases & vapors, that it is primordial, reproductive, & sexy. As far as his thinking 'language is a virus,' that is his entitlement. For myself, language is language & a virus is a virus. When one attempts to reduce something to something else, you risk obscuring/diluting the something you're transferring, robbing it of its indigenous integrity. Additionally, I don't believe language requires a host as a virus does.

Recently I've been focused on what I call the Linguistically Undocumented which refers to a word's under-recognized, marginal, border-line status. By submitting a word like LURK to multiple modules/formulations thereby provoking multiple exfoliations, the word appears fleshified, muscularized, densified as it evolves & matures. Hopefully, after a reader experiences over fifty LURK behaviorisms, they will become more intimate with the term. When they hear or see the word a bell of recognition will go off, their rapport with LURK will have enriched their world much as a birder studying a cardinal for months will feel that they now have a rapprochement with the cardinal, with their song, their mating & nesting habits, their postural dispositions.

This is part of the campaign. To awaken persons to the Universe, to free ourselves from the culture of measurement & classification, to embrace the Immeasurably Incalculable.

DCW: **You also study animal behavior. Which sounds quite fascinating, and I imagine there are many parallels with your work away from and with the pen. Could you please elaborate on some of these parallels? Differences?**

HL: That's actually funny. When I moved to NYC from Los Angeles about 15 years ago, surrounded by a preponderance of human animals, it seemed like a perfect opportunity to learn more about my fellow creature, so, somewhat flippantly, I added that to my bio. No one has ever asked me what animal(s) I was studying.

Less flippantly, I have had some deep experiences with canines. In L.A., I helped train dogs for the sheriff's department, principally in the area of scent & protection work. I also competed in the German dog sport of *shutzhund*. In New York I worked with a 2 dog team in protection training (there is a video of this on youtube with over 1.4million views… ironically, my poetry readings average 100 views).

My work with canines has indeed been one of the deep privileges I've been gifted. I will shy from your word 'parallels' as parallels do not 'touch' & substitute fuse/intercourse with.

The animals taught (& continue to teach) deep humility because they are so sensitive, emotive, & canny. It exacerbates that Universities spend millions of dollars measuring (again that 'measuring' reflex) a dog's intelligence with testing, calculations, studies, etc. What a waste of time & money! Anyone with any experience with dogs & animals know they are intelligent. One study shows that a mature dog can understand as many English words as a 7 year old. My experience indicates that a dog can pretty much understand whatever you have to say. With my 2 dog team (Emily & Nietzsche), I had only to think a thought & they would react. I did not even have to issue a command. I have rarely experienced that level of telepathic intensity. Who are we to rate a dog's intelligence? How do you rate their olfactory intelligence? There are multiple intelligences & to try to format intelligence in accordance with our scale of values is to demean the universe around us.

A great Hinge event is cross-species intercourse. Intercourse here is used in the large sense of communication & mutual dealings. Dealing with animals is a wonderful spiritual exercise in excising the ego, . . . you can't approach the essence of the 'other' if you are still self-entangled.

DCW: **Through our discussions over the years, it has been made clear that music has an important role in your creativity. What are you listening to these days? How has your relationship with music impacted your relationship with words, with language?**

HL: The second part of your question elicits differing response-approaches. The normative reflex would be to list & delineate the various ways in which music has impacted my poetic practice, e.g., 'Trane's use of the augmented triad in the first chorus of "One down, One Up," shifted my imagistic relations while Elvin's cascading triplet patterns suggested new possibilities for how line disjunction could enhance percussive power.'

This would be a slight response. By parceling & peeling-off slices of influence I would be betraying the enormity of influence. Sure, I could itemize & say that I consider Eric Dolphy my poetic mentor, as I tried to emulate his sonic with my linguistic, that musicians such as Dizzy, Brownie, Jackie McClean, Horace Silver, Blakey, Bill Evans, Pharoah Sanders, Jim Hall, Wes, Trane, among others, changed my world as well as tunes like 'Three Blind Mice,' 'Delilah,' 'Love Supreme,' 'Passin' Thru,' 'Kulu Se Mama,' 'Song For My Father,' 'One Down, One Up,' & I'd just be getting started.

But rather than pointing to an A/B causal relationship, e.g., Blakey's press roll taught me how to develop line sustain, a vaster more fusionist approach asserts that *I am my assimilations*. From this perspective, all my life events inter(mingle)(course) fecundate rotate & flux in creative ekstasis. I use the term 'event' rather than 'experience' because 'event' permits amalgam & does not preference a subject as having undergone the 'experience.'

The short answer, then, to "how has your relationship with music impacted your relationship with words, with language?" would be: Yes, it has. But more precisely then 'impacted,' which sets up a binary division between music & my poetry, would be to say that music has fused/merged been assimilated/absorbed into my self, the being that I am. Included in that assimilation would also be artists – Giacometti, Cezanne, Van Gogh, Soutine, Agnes Martin, Pollock, Franz Klein, Linda Lynch, to name a few – as well as canines, certain oak, cherry & birch trees, the brook in my backyard, thunderstorms, twilight & so forth. Nothing is alien. This is the Great Cosmic Smooch. The intercrackling rainbow warble fluting from whale brow. To isolate & sort so I can say this relationship produced this result is simply not applicable. To simplify through reduction sucks out the Savor, destitutes Sapience.

Recently I've been listening to a lot of 50's & 60's jazz as well as songbirds. I live in the woods & the birdsong this year has been unusually fertile.

DCW: **What was one gratifying thing that was said to you, in relation to and/or following the release of LURK?**

HL: One gratifying comment that was emailed to me:
"I started reading LURK out loud, as is my wont, and my Polish sweetheart's boy said to me *'what is that, some sort of incantation?' You see how attuned youth can be!*" ■

The originator of Hinge Theory, HELLER LEVINSON lives in New York.

BLACK WIDOW PRESS :: POETRY IN TRANSLATION

Approximate Man and Other Writings by Tristan Tzara. Translated and edited by Mary Ann Caws.

Art Poétique by Guillevic. Translated by Maureen Smith.

Beginnings of the Prose Poem. Edited by Mary Ann Caws, Michel Delville.

The Big Game by Benjamin Péret. Translated with an introduction by Marilyn Kallet.

Boris Vian Invents Boris Vian: A Boris Vian Reader. Edited and translated by Julia Older.

Capital of Pain by Paul Eluard. Translated by Mary Ann Caws, Patricia Terry, and Nancy Kline.

Chanson Dada: Selected Poems by Tristan Tzara. Translated with an introduction and essay by Lee Harwood.

Earthlight (Clair de Terre) by André Breton. Translated by Bill Zavatsky and Zack Rogow. (New & revised ed.)

Essential Poems and Prose of Jules Laforgue. Translated and edited by Patricia Terry.

Essential Poems and Writings of Joyce Mansour: A Bilingual Anthology. Translated with an introduction by Serge Gavronsky.

Essential Poems and Writings of Robert Desnos: A Bilingual Anthology. Edited with an introduction and essay by Mary Ann Caws.

EyeSeas (Les Ziaux) by Raymond Queneau. Translated with an introduction by Daniela Hurezanu and Stephen Kessler.

Fables in a Modern Key by Pierre Coran. Translated by Norman R. Shapiro. Full-color illustrations by Olga Pastuchiv.

Fables of Town & Country by Pierre Coran. Translated by Norman R. Shapiro. Full-color illustrations by Olga Pastuchiv.

A Flea the Size of Paris: The Old French Fatrasies & Fatras. Edited and translated by Ted Byrne and Donato Mancini.

Forbidden Pleasures: New Selected Poems 1924–1949 by Luis Cernuda. Translated by Stephen Kessler.

Furor and Mystery & Other Writings by René Char. Translated by Mary Ann Caws and Nancy Kline.

The Gentle Genius of Cécile Périn: Selected Poems (1906–1956). Edited and translated by Norman R. Shapiro.

The Great Madness by Avigdor Hameiri. Translated and edited by Peter C. Appelbaum with an introduction by Dan Hecht.

Guarding the Air: Selected Poems of Gunnar Harding. Translated & edited by Roger Greenwald.

Howls & Growls: French Poems to Bark By. Translated by Norman R. Shapiro; illustrated by Olga K. Pastuchiv.

I Have Invented Nothing: Selected Poems by Jean-Pierre Rosnay. Translated by J. Kates.

In Praise of Sleep: Selected Poems of Lucian Blaga. Translated with an introduction by Andrei Codrescu.

The Inventor of Love & Other Writings by Gherasim Luca. Translated by Julian & Laura Semilian. Introduction by Andrei Codrescu. Essay by Petre Răileanu.

Jules Supervielle: Selected Prose and Poetry. Translated by Nancy Kline & Patricia Terry.

La Fontaine's Bawdy by Jean de La Fontaine. Translated with an introduction by Norman R. Shapiro.

Last Love Poems of Paul Eluard. Translated with an introduction by Marilyn Kallet.

A Life of Poems, Poems of a Life by Anna de Noailles. Edited and translated by Norman R. Shapiro. Introduction by Catherine Perry.

Love, Poetry (L'amour la poésie) by Paul Eluard. Translated with an essay by Stuart Kendall.

Of Human Carnage—Odessa 1918–1920 by Avigdor Hameiri. Translated and edited by Peter C. Appelbaum with an introduction by Dan Hecht.

Pierre Reverdy: Poems, Early to Late. Translated by Mary Ann Caws and Patricia Terry.

Poems of André Breton: A Bilingual Anthology. Translated with essays by Jean-Pierre Cauvin and Mary Ann Caws.

Poems of A.O. Barnabooth by Valery Larbaud. Translated by Ron Padgett and Bill Zavatsky.

Poems of Consummation by Vicente Aleixandre. Translated by Stephen Kessler.

Préversities: A Jacques Prévert Sampler. Translated and edited by Norman R. Shapiro.

RhymAmusings (AmuseRimes) by Pierre Coran. Translated by Norman R. Shapiro.

The Sea and Other Poems by Guillevic. Translated by Patricia Terry. Introduction by Monique Chefdor.

Sixty Years: Selected Poems 1957–2017 by Mikhail Yeryomin. Translated by J. Kates.

Through Naked Branches by Tarjei Vesaas. Translated, edited, and introduced by Roger Greenwald.

To Speak, to Tell You? Poems by Sabine Sicaud. Translated by Norman R. Shapiro. Introduction and notes by Odile Ayral-Clause.

BLACK WIDOW PRESS :: MODERN POETRY SERIES

WILLIS BARNSTONE
ABC of Translation
African Bestiary (Forthcoming)

DAVE BRINKS
The Caveat Onus
The Secret Brain: Selected Poems 1995–2012

RUXANDRA CESEREANU
Crusader-Woman. Translated by Adam J. Sorkin. Introduction by Andrei Codrescu.
Forgiven Submarine by Ruxandra Cesereanu and Andrei Codrescu.

CLAYTON ESHLEMAN
An Alchemist with One Eye on Fire
Anticline
Archaic Design
Clayton Eshleman/The Essential Poetry: 1960–2015
Grindstone of Rapport: A Clayton Eshleman Reader
Penetralia
Pollen Aria
The Price of Experience
Endure: Poems by Bei Dao. Translated by Clayton Eshleman and Lucas Klein.
Curdled Skulls: Poems of Bernard Bador. Translated by Bernard Bador with Clayton Eshleman.

PIERRE JORIS
Barzakh (Poems 2000–2012)
Exile Is My Trade: A Habib Tengour Reader

MARILYN KALLET
Even When We Sleep
How Our Bodies Learned
Packing Light: New and Selected Poems
The Love That Moves Me
Disenchanted City (La ville désenchantée) by Chantal Bizzini. Translated by J. Bradford Anderson, Darren Jackson, and Marilyn Kallet.

ROBERT KELLY
Fire Exit
The Hexagon

STEPHEN KESSLER
Garage Elegies
Last Call

BILL LAVENDER
Memory Wing

HELLER LEVINSON
from stone this running
LinguaQuake
Lure
Lurk
jus' sayn'
Seep
Tenebraed
Un-
Wrack Lariat

JOHN OLSON
Backscatter: New and Selected Poems
Dada Budapest
Larynx Galaxy
Weave of the Dream King

NIYI OSUNDARE
City Without People: The Katrina Poems
Green: Sighs of Our Ailing Planet: Poems

MEBANE ROBERTSON
An American Unconscious
Signal from Draco: New and Selected Poems

JEROME ROTHENBERG
Concealments and Caprichos
Eye of Witness: A Jerome Rothenberg Reader. Edited with commentaries by Heriberto Yepez & Jerome Rothenberg.
The President of Desolation & Other Poems

AMINA SAÏD
The Present Tense of the World: Poems 2000–2009. Translated with an introduction by Marilyn Hacker.

ANIS SHIVANI
Soraya (Sonnets)

JERRY W. WARD, JR.
Fractal Song

BLACK WIDOW PRESS :: ANTHOLOGIES / BIOGRAPHIES

Barbaric Vast & Wild: A Gathering of Outside and Subterranean Poetry (*Poems for the Millennium*, vol. 5). Jerome Rothenberg and John Bloomberg-Rissman, editors.

Clayton Eshleman: The Whole Art by Stuart Kendall

Revolution of the Mind: The Life of André Breton by Mark Polizzotti